Original title:
Bracelets of Love

Copyright © 2025 Creative Arts Management OÜ
All rights reserved.

Author: Lorenzo Barrett
ISBN HARDBACK: 978-1-80586-208-6
ISBN PAPERBACK: 978-1-80586-680-0

Whispered Promises

In a drawer they're hidden, shiny and bright,
With charms that giggle, oh what a sight!
They twist and they tangle, a friendship's delight,
Each clip tells a tale, oh what fun at night!

A tiny heart dances, a cat with a grin,
When worn just right, it draws all the win.
They jingle and jangle, on each little limb,
A fashion statement, or just a whim!

When friends come together, they trade with such glee,
A sprinkle of laughter, a pinch of esprit.
They wear them with pride as they sip on their tea,
Unraveling stories as wild as can be!

So here's to the trinkets, that shimmer and shine,
With giggles and joy, oh how they align!
In the game of friendship, they twirl and they climb,
Forever reminding us, life's moments are prime!

Memories Wrapped Tight

Worn like secrets in a twist,
Each charm a giggle, can't resist.
When friends come round, we laugh and play,
Those little trinkets save the day.

With every clasp, a tale unfolds,
Of silly dances and stories told.
Each bead a memory, bold and bright,
Wrapped in friendship, held so tight.

Adorned in Love's Palette

Colors clash and patterns bleep,
Silly treasures, no need to weep.
A jumble of joy on our wrists,
Each hue a wink, a playful twist.

From neon greens to sparkly reds,
They bounce around like bouncing heads.
Our laughter echoes in the night,
Adorned with colors, pure delight.

Embracing Possibilities

A twist here, a turn there, the fun begins,
With every clasp, we spark new wins.
Looping dreams through little holes,
Each jingle brightens up our souls.

Expect the best, embrace the chance,
With silly bands, we start to dance.
Holding close the silly glee,
In every twist, there's you and me.

Lattice of Love

Woven patterns, a tangled spree,
A lattice made for absurdity.
Bangles jingle in the sun,
Together, we embrace the fun.

Each charm a laugh, a clever pun,
A twist of fate, we're never done.
In silly styles, our hearts ignite,
A jolly weave, our joy in sight.

Curvature of Care

In a world where colors twist,
My wrist twirls with a blissful tryst.
Beads of laughter float and sway,
Making monkeys dance and play.

Every charm is quirky, bold,
Stories shared of young and old.
A flick, a twist, a playful pull,
Together we can make it full.

Sparkling Sentiments

A jingle here, a jangle there,
My arm's a circus, full of flair.
Glittering gems, all out of tune,
Bow ties and bananas croon a tune.

From frilly hearts to tiny frogs,
Each bauble hums, like happy dogs.
With each bump and each embrace,
We turn the world into a race.

Vertices of Affinity

In friendship's knot we find our groove,
Plenty of nonsense helps us move.
Geometric fun on every bend,
A twisty bond that will not end.

Triangles and squares, we draw them loud,
Laughing at the mess, feeling proud.
With shapes we patch our quirkiest tales,
As smiles and giggles set the sails.

Unfolding Ties

Wrap around my wrist, just so,
A tumble of joy, a colorful show.
Each loop, a chuckle, a wink, a cheer,
Crafting moments that bring us near.

Pull a thread, see what unfurls,
A ribbon of giggles, and friendship swirls.
Swapping woes while sipping tea,
Together we're the best tipple spree.

Chains of Affection

In a world of shiny things,
We wear our quirks like bling.
A heavy chain or dainty rope,
Each jingle brings a laugh and hope.

When my friend trips in her gold,
We giggle loud, her tales retold.
A charm that dangles, oh so bright,
It makes her dance in pure delight.

Adornments of Emotion

Links that sparkle, links that twist,
Every catch a twist of mist.
We trade our tales in gentle jest,
In this odd parade, we feel the best.

A gem that's chipped, a bead that's gone,
Each piece of flair, a silly song.
I wear your laughter on my wrist,
In this odd dance, we still persist.

Threads of Togetherness

Woven tightly, but often loose,
Our antics shine, a joyful ruse.
A faded string once thought so bright,
It holds our giggles, day and night.

Tangled up in tales we share,
A cozy bond that fills the air.
A little fray brings out our style,
We wear it proudly, laugh a while.

Whispers of Connection

With every clasp, a secret's spun,
A gentle nudge, we play for fun.
The magic's found in every clasp,
In this wild game, together we gasp.

A worn-out string, now frayed and sweet,
It tells our stories with every beat.
With every giggle, bond so true,
In our collection, there's always room for you.

Gems of Affection

In a box of glitzy charms,
Products of our silly harms,
Each one tells a goofy tale,
Of clumsy falls and ice cream trails.

They dangle, sparkle, catch the eye,
Laughing at the times gone by,
A glitter here, a wink from there,
Memories made with love and flair.

Resilient Revelries

Worn through laughter, worn through tears,
A testament to all our years,
They bend but never break, you see,
Like our dance moves — oh so free!

Colors clash like our bad jokes,
Together still, we're just two folks,
With each clasp a giggling fit,
In our world, we firmly sit.

Enduring Links

Links of laughter, links of fun,
They twist and turn, then come undone,
A chain of chaos, brightly bright,
In friendship's bond, we delight!

Stretching wide, then tightening small,
We celebrate the silly call,
In every twist, a little cheer,
With every stone, a memory dear.

Merging Melodies

Notes of laughter, sweet and clear,
Each chime a jest we hold so dear,
Mingling tones, both high and low,
In melodies of love, we glow.

Dance and twirl, the music plays,
We blend our quirks in funky ways,
A symphony of joyful glee,
In harmony, just you and me.

Circles of Embrace

In circles round our wrists, we laugh,
As charms jingle, the silly half.
With twinkling eyes, we swap a glance,
These shiny rings lead to a dance.

They're like hugs that never squeeze,
Brightening days with playful tease.
Each sparkly charm a story told,
In this game of love, we break the mold.

Trinkets of Devotion

Trinkets upon our arms parade,
Each one a memory we've made.
A cupcake charm for a sweet mishap,
These playful gifts make love a snap.

Finger food in a golden clasp,
A wink and laugh, a silly gasp.
With every clink, our spirits rise,
Surrounded by laughter, it's no surprise.

Gems of Connection

Gems that glitter and catch the light,
Making friendships feel just right.
A pineapple charm for summertime fun,
In this goofy game, we're never done.

With every gem, a story stirs,
Like silly dances, and tumbling furs.
We wear our laughter like a crown,
Each little piece turns frowns upside down.

Woven Whispers

Whispers woven in colors bright,
A sneaky charm jumps in the night.
Each little trinket spins a tale,
Of goofy things that never fail.

Like socks on hands or silly hats,
These fibrous threads connect the facts.
In every twist, a giggle shared,
With woven love, we're truly paired.

Tokens of Lasting Bond

In the drawer, they lie and wait,
A blingy mess, oh such a fate!
Looping and tangled in a dance,
They giggle at my clumsy chance.

Each charm tells tales, a bit absurd,
Of coffee spills and jokes that stirred.
Jingling with laughter as I pass,
A clink, a clash, oh what a brass!

Circles of Sweet Memory

Round and round, they twinkle bright,
A collection of giggles, what a sight!
One with a cat, another a shoe,
Each tells a story, funny and true.

I wear them high, like a crown so bold,
But watch out, they may just scold!
"Too many friends!" I hear them sing,
Who knew adornments could cause such bling?

Emblems of Enchantment

A trinket here, a doodad there,
Each has a goofy little flare.
One grins wide, the other cries,
Who knew metal could hold such highs?

In puzzling patterns, they overlap,
Creating chaos, a shiny trap.
With every jingle, a chuckle flies,
My silly charms under the skies.

Embraced by Adornment

Wrapped in shimmer, I prance around,
A walking jester, what a sound!
My wrist's a stage, a circus of cheer,
Performing fights with each chatter near.

They clash and smile, a playful crew,
Teasing me like the best of you.
Together we laugh, oh what a scene,
A quirky fashion, quite the routine!

Memory's Embrace

In a drawer I found a band,
Dusty, twisted, and oh so grand.
I wore it once, just for a show,
Now it clings to my wrist like a crow.

My cat stole it, ran up a tree,
Chased by squirrels, oh woe is me!
With a flick of the tail, it took a dive,
Now it's the fashion of the feline tribe.

It glimmers in the evening sun,
With every giggle, we're back to fun.
A story told, a laugh we share,
In this tangled mess, love's always fair.

Though it may lack a shiny grace,
It holds the warmth of a silly face.
With each loop and twist it makes,
It's the ride of life that laughter takes.

Love's Artistry

We crafted our bands from candy wrappers,
With sticky fingers and endless chappers.
Wore them proudly, like kings and queens,
Till they melted away in our ice cream scenes.

My friend's turned green from the chewing gum,
A masterpiece that's oh so glum.
Yet every twist, and every turn,
Brings back smiles and lessons learned.

During rainy days, we danced about,
With paper chains that made us shout.
Each drizzle laughed while we tried to skip,
With our art on display, love's funny trip.

So here's to the crafts of our youth,
Adventurous, silly, and filled with truth.
These wacky wonders, though frayed and old,
Wear the tales of laughter we've told.

Luster of Togetherness

Wearing mismatched socks, we twirl and play,
With shiny beads jingling all day.
Our laughter sparkles, not made of gold,
But treasures of fun that never grow old.

In a race, we lost a charm or two,
But with each step, our giggles grew.
A necklace now, or perhaps a ring?
Who cares when it's laughter we bring?

With ice cream stains upon our hands,
We built our dreams on shifting sands.
A luster that shines in the moonlit night,
Where silly dances feel just right.

These moments shimmer, imperfect but bright,
In a world where love finds laughter's light.
A whimsical twist, in all that we weave,
Is the joy of togetherness we believe.

Adorning Affection

I thought of love as a shiny trinket,
But found a sock that's now a pinket.
Swapped rings for rubber bands, just for fun,
Creating treasures beneath the sun.

Decorated cups with our scribbled dreams,
Overflowing with milkshakes and silly screams.
Each sip a giggle, each bite a laugh,
Who needs jewels when we have our craft?

Our silly strings twine tight around,
In this goofy dance, we are spellbound.
Each snicker shared is a bracelet in disguise,
Adorning our wrists, much to our surprise.

So here's to the quirks that make us whole,
With laughter and love, it's a funny role.
Through silly crafts and delightful play,
We find affection in our own quirky way.

The Binding Spirit

Once I bought a gift so bright,
A shiny charm, a pure delight.
Thought it'd make my love feel great,
But it slipped right off—what a fate!

We laugh and joke, it's quite a scene,
A twinkling trinket, fit for a queen.
It bounced around like a playful pup,
Then rolled away—Oh, pick it up!

Trinkets of Devotion

I tied a string around my wrist,
To show my love, I couldn't resist.
But every time I wave hello,
It flings off fast, like a rodeo!

My partner giggles, calls it a sport,
This rubber band we feel is cute and short.
It snaps and zings like a rubber chick,
Love in motion, what a funny trick!

Jewelry of the Heart

Got a necklace that says "You're mine!"
But I forgot to check the design.
Now tangled in my hair it lies,
A lumpy jumble—much to my surprise!

We laugh about this fashion craze,
A shining heart that's gone astray.
"Next time," I vow, "I'll do it right,"
But love's a mess, and that's alright!

Encircled by Warmth

A circle of gold around my arm,
Thought it'd keep my love from harm.
But it slipped off in a grand ballet,
Now it's stuck on the neighbor's stray!

"Hey, come back!" I shout and scream,
As my heart dances and starts to dream.
Yet as I chase, we burst with glee,
What a wild tangled spree!

Essence of Embrace

In a store full of charms, a lady did roam,
She found one that sparkled, it felt like home.
Her dog tried to nibble, that cheeky young mutt,
He thought it's a snack, oh what a big glut!

With laughter galore, she turned to her friend,
"Socks and jewelry, the fashion will blend!"
But each time she wore it, her wrist lost some space,
With donuts and cupcakes, it lost its fine grace.

Design of the Heart

A pendant of jellybeans, so bright and so sweet,
Who knew love had flavors, such a tasty treat?
But as it hung lower, it knocked on her knee,
"Is this romance? Or did I just trip over me?"

She designed it with sparkles, and glitter galore,
Despite looking lovely, it twinkled and swore!
Grab my wrist if you want, but do mind the stash,
I'm adorned with snacks that can cause quite a clash!

Harmony in Adornment

A rainbow of buttons she wore on her arm,
Each button a memory, each one with its charm.
Her friends started giggling, "What's with the bling?"
"Oh dear darlings, it's fashion, I'm practically a king!"

And when she danced wildly, her buttons took flight,
They twanged on her wrist like a band in the night.
"Is this love on my arm, or an orchestra's play?"
She laughed as they jangled and danced all the way.

Aureate Affections

He wore all his best bling, to impress a fine dame,
A golden attire, oh what a grand game!
But with every bold step, his wrist started to creak,
Was this love he was feeling? Or just a sore peak?

As she caught her eye, he tripped on a chair,
And his jewels flew off, like they simply don't care!
"I offer my heart, but it seems like a bust,
Love with lost jewelry? Oh, that's a great thrust!"

Simple Sentiments

A shiny band around my wrist,
It sparkles more than I insist.
A gift from you, my goofy friend,
It represents the laughs we send.

We wear them proudly, side by side,
They're like a chat, just bona fide.
If lost, I'd search without a doubt,
For all the giggles we're about.

A twist of fate brought us so near,
Each charm exchanged brings us more cheer.
A tiny heart, a jester's hat,
The memories wrapped like a cat.

So here's to us, those silly ties,
With each small gift, the joy just flies.
We'll wear these jewels with quite a flair,
The laughs and love are everywhere.

Linking Hearts

A charm that jingles, oh so bright,
Like friends who dance in the soft light.
Each link a chuckle, each bead a jest,
In goofy moments, we are blessed.

You lost a piece, oh what a scene!
In search we went, you know what I mean.
We saw a dog with such a flair,
And borrowed from him without a care.

With every jing, it tells a tale,
Of silly days where we prevail.
Your laughter echoes, sweet and loud,
These tokens wrap us in a shroud.

Like strands of pasta, twisted and fun,
Together we shine brighter than the sun.
Each gift we trade, a wink, a nod,
In this grand play, we both applaud.

Tangled Emotions

Oh why's my wrist a jumble mess?
This charm's a puzzle I must confess.
A whale beside a tiny shoe,
Represents the wild things we've been through.

When I pull one, they all come too,
Like friends who gather when we brew.
Each charm's a giggle, even a grin,
Conversations sparked with a tiny spin.

"Did you see that?!" I stretch the strand,
It expands like dreams oh so grand.
But tangled love, it does confound,
Our laughter, though, knows no bound.

Each gift whispers secrets, light yet bold,
Of memories past and treasures told.
We wear our joy, a wild array,
These funny trinkets come out to play.

Souvenirs of Serenity

Here's a trinket shaped like a fish,
It's not as graceful as I'd wish.
But every swirl's a laugh we share,
A treasure found with loving care.

A tiny bell that never rings,
Yet in my heart, its humor sings.
A quirky charm that seems to smile,
Makes every moment feel worthwhile.

You gave me one that looks like cake,
I laugh so hard, I might just break.
Though dessert's a dream I can't fulfill,
This tiny charm brings such a thrill.

So here we stand with friendship's thread,
These quirky charms, like laughter fed.
In joy we find our greatest peace,
With silly gifts, the fun won't cease.

Shimmering Promises

In a store that's oh-so-bright,
I spotted something, what a sight!
A shiny band that sparkled clear,
I thought, now this belongs to dear.

But as I tried it on my wrist,
It slipped away, oh what a twist!
It bounced around the floor like fate,
I swear these jewels must set a date!

I chased it down, a dance to find,
The shopkeeper laughed, 'Get in line!'
With every leap, my heart went thump,
For love's not just a shiny lump.

Yet in the end, we both agreed,
A charm for you is what you need.
Though laughter echoed through the roam,
We'll wear our treasures when we're home.

Touch of Forever

A bracelet made of gummy bears,
I gave to you, amid our stares.
You laughed and said it's quite the treat,
But on your wrist, it smelled like feet!

We giggled as we took a stroll,
Each bear fell out, oh dear, what a toll!
You stopped to scoop them one by one,
'This love is messy, but oh so fun!'

With sticky hands and faces bright,
We ate the candy, what a sight!
A sugar-high, a swirly spin,
Our laughter echoed, pure and thin.

So here's to love that's sweet and strange,
In every giggle, life will change.
Forever's just a joke, you see,
With every bear, it's you and me!

Sealed Affections

In a box with bows so grand,
I found a gift—you'd love it, man!
A ring of shells, a beachy flair,
But then it broke, and oh, the despair!

I tried to seal it with some glue,
But ended up with sticky goo.
My fingers stuck, my heart still bold,
A true love story, yet untold.

You laughed and said, 'You're quite the mess!'
Yet from this chaos, we are blessed.
For every seal that comes undone,
Is just a chance to laugh and run!

So here's our love, a crazy art,
With broken shells, yet whole in heart.
In every slip and every fall,
We'll dance together, through it all!

Links of Shared Dreams

I saw a chain that caught my eye,
It promised dreams and made me sigh.
I bought it quick, how could I know,
It tangled up in quite the show?

We sat and pulled, a tug of war,
Like cats and yarn, we wanted more!
The links were strong, but love's a twist,
In all this chaos, we can't resist.

We laughed so hard, it hurt our sides,
In every twist, a love that glides.
Unlinked or linked, we're still a pair,
With every clash, we show we care.

So here's to dreams that intertwine,
In every knot, our hearts align.
With laughter shared, we'll always gleam,
Together we'll fulfill our dream!

Braid of Heartstrings

Two hearts stringing laughter,
With knots that slip and slide.
Each loop tells a joke,
As we dance side by side.

A bead of mischief rolls,
And pops with such delight.
We giggle as we scramble,
To find it in the night.

Our threads may tangle up,
Like spaghetti on a plate.
But in this crazy weave,
It's love that we create.

The patterns twist and turn,
In colors bright and bold.
We wear our silly joys,
Like treasures to behold.

Adorned in Trust

A charm for every blunder,
Each slip-up has a tale.
We wear our goof-ups proud,
With laughter, we prevail.

A golden wink of faith,
As we trip over a shoe.
Trust is the shiny clasp,
That secures this crazy crew.

In this jangle of mishaps,
Our humor's here to stay.
We sport a smile each day,
In the most absurd way.

With every twist and turn,
We find our silly spark.
Adorned in trust and fun,
We'll chase away the dark.

Interwoven Sentiments

Threads of thoughts entwined,
In patterns oh so bright.
We stitch together dreams,
In the shimmer of moonlight.

Witty words like pearls,
Dangle from our chatter.
Each laugh is a treasure,
In this friendship's platter.

When hearts begin to merge,
And spark a silly grin,
It's like combining socks,
That somehow still fit in.

With every twist and turn,
We revel in our art.
Interwoven sentiments,
Will never drift apart.

Fastened Futures

A clasp that holds the jokes,
And binds our hopes so tight.
Each funny little moment,
Glimmers in the light.

We fasten every dream,
With ribbons of the past.
What matters is the laughter,
That forever will last.

As time slips through our fingers,
And life becomes a game,
We tie up silly wishes,
And call them by our name.

In every twist we take,
The future's bright and clear.
Our bonds are full of giggles,
And love that's always near.

Rings of Unity

In a world where we're tied by a twist,
Some call it fashion, we call it bliss.
With bling on our wrists, we dance around,
I lost one—oh look! It's safe and sound.

Jewelry jangles to the beat of our cheer,
Each sparkling gem holds a giggle near.
We trade them like cards, 'Oh, take mine today!'
Just don't ask me where that last one may stay.

Matching pieces, we wander like fools,
A treasure hunt game, breaking all rules.
If I wear a heart, you wear a star,
Together we shine, no matter how far.

In this bracelet of gleeful delight,
We wrap up our troubles, our laughter takes flight.
With each twist and turn, we'll flaunt and we'll tease,
In this circus of love, we do as we please.

Embers of Loyalty

In the mix of charms, we find our way,
A laugh and a wink, we seize the day.
Our outfits are wild, like our friendship is,
With charm bracelets tucked in a stylish fizz.

Each charm tells a tale, some silly, some bright,
Like the time we got lost on a gnome-chase at night.
With our obsessions stitched tight, we giggled all night,
Two peas in a pod, what a goofy sight!

We'll stick together, come rain or come shine,
With glittery gadgets that glimmer and shine.
In loyal delight, we dance in a whirl,
'Just don't break my charm! It's my favorite pearl!'

So here's to the knots that we tie and we weave,
In this colorful web of joy, we believe.
For as long as they jingle, our spirits will soar,
With the glow of our quirks, we'll always want more.

Lovelocks in the Twilight

In a twilight glow, where whispers entwine,
Our tinkling treasures, like old vintage wine.
Each lock tells our secrets, our giggles, our sighs,
Who knew lovelocks could lead to such highs?

As the moon winks down, we clink and we clank,
A symphony made from the charms we thank.
If one goes missing, don't you shed a tear,
It'll turn up behind the sofa, I fear!

Adventures unravel like threads of a dream,
While tangled in laughter, we plot and we scheme.
With each silly trinket and shimmer of gold,
We stitch up a story, silly yet bold.

So here's to the charms that swing with our song,
We'll laugh through the night, all the way 'til dawn.
In this constellation of quirks and delight,
Our lovelocks are shining, a comical sight!

Cuffs of Companionship

Wrist to wrist, we're a goofy pair,
Cuffs that connect us, not just in despair.
With mismatched charms all clinking away,
If one hits the floor, we'll giggle and play.

In silly situations, we find our refrain,
Like the time we wore shades in a pouring rain.
We laugh till we cry, what a ridiculous show,
With wrist cuffs so bright, our friendship will glow.

So when life gets tough, we give it a twist,
In our laughter, we find what others have missed.
Two pals on a journey, with cuffs that unite,
Through chaos and fun, we'll keep it alight.

With giggles and charms, our fun won't be tamed,
Forever in cuffs, together unframed.
In this quirk of life, let's frolic and roam,
For with you by my side, I always feel home.

Emblems of Endearment

Around my wrist, a shiny band,
It jingles loud, I proudly stand.
A partner's joke, a wink, a tease,
We laugh together, hearts at ease.

Each charm a tale, a silly grin,
A tale of love infused with kin.
Tickles and nudges, we can't resist,
In this silly game, I can't be missed.

Like popcorn kernels, we pop and sway,
In playful chaos, we find our way.
Each clink a chime of laughter's tune,
Together we dance, morning to noon.

Through ups and downs, we prance about,
Our colorful charms, there's never doubt.
In the circus of love, we take our seat,
With every giggle, life's bittersweet.

Mementos in Motion

A twist and turn, my wrist does spin,
Every little charm, a tickled grin.
With each little jingle, joy's alive,
We're two goofy clowns, we laugh and thrive.

A tiny frog leaps, a fish that swims,
Our memories dance, with playful whims.
Each charm a memory, oh what a mix,
Like juggling cats and balancing tricks.

In moments of daftness, we take great care,
We trip on laughter, it's everywhere.
With knots of giggles and threads of fun,
Life's a carnival, come join the run.

Twirling with joy, what a silly spree,
Our hearts aligned, as light as can be.
The magic we wear, blinged and bright,
Together we shine, oh what a sight!

Connection's Caress

Each twist of my wrist, a laugh unfurls,
A dance of love where chaos twirls.
My necklace sways, a bright parade,
We're like merry bees, no plans are laid.

This jolly vibe connects us tight,
A slapstick duo, day and night.
Like magnets drawn, we can't hold still,
In silly snaps, we find our thrill.

Clinking and clanking, we're quite the pair,
In every chuckle, a loving flare.
Our shared moments, just like confetti,
Sprinkled with joy, always ready.

So here's to us, in zany delight,
Forever tangled, our hearts take flight.
With laughter and charm, we won't confuse,
Life's a stage, let's amuse and cruise!

Harmonious Threads

A twist of fabric wrought in glee,
Our silly antics, a melody.
With every tug, our joy is free,
In yarns of laughter, you and me.

Colors that clash yet flow so bright,
Together we weave day into night.
Connecting hearts with needle and thread,
In this wacky quilt, silly tales spread.

The patterns dance, a vibrance so bold,
A tapestry spun with stories retold.
With every loop, our bond grows wide,
A joyful journey, side by side.

So raise a glass, let's toast the spree,
Life's a patchwork of you and me.
In this carnival of love and art,
We stitch together with giggles at heart.

Interwoven Stories

In a twisty world, we laugh and twine,
Threads of our stories, oh how they shine.
A silly dance, as we giggle and tease,
These loops of joy, they often appease.

With charms that jingle and beads that glow,
Our silly secrets in tow, we bestow.
Each color a tale, we weave through the night,
Laughter is caught, oh what a delight!

We swap our trinkets without any care,
Each one a treasure, a memory to share.
With knots and quirks, we build our own way,
These goofy tales, in our hearts, they stay.

So here's to the fun, and the bonds that we make,
With every twist, a ridiculous take.
In this fabric of life, we thread our own song,
United in laughter, where we all belong.

Shimmering Connections

In a world that sparkles, we dance and spin,
With shiny baubles that match our grin.
A wink and a nod, as we flicker our charms,
These connections we make, keep us safe from harms.

Little treasures twirl in a joyful ballet,
Each laugh echoing, bursting like clay.
With stories that shimmer, each moment we flaunt,
Our goofy ensemble, a delightful jaunt.

Through loops of laughter, we spark and ignite,
With dreams in each color, our hearts feel so bright.
Oh, the blunders we cherish, they light up the day,
In this quirky connection, we giggle away.

So let's twinkle together, with every misfit,
In a dance of delight, let our spirits commit.
With goofy connections that sparkle like stars,
We pen our own tales, without any bars.

Symphony of Sentiments

In a mad orchestra, we each find our tune,
With laughs and mishaps, we sing to the moon.
Every note that we play, a memory in flight,
This symphony grows with each silly delight.

The trumpets of friendship blast loud and clear,
While giggles crescendo, oh how we cheer.
Each stride a misstep, each laugh a surprise,
In this quirky concerto, we soar to the skies.

Our melodies mingle, a dance so rare,
With harmonies tangled, we weave through the air.
A chorus of laughter, a funny refrain,
This symphony echoes in sunshine and rain.

So hold tight the music, let's dance and sway,
In this riot of feelings, we'll play all day.
With rhythms of joy, our hearts scream aloud,
In this symphony, we'll always be proud.

Threads of Remembrance

Through tangled yarn, our laughter gets spun,
Each quirky moment, a tangle of fun.
We tug at our memories, pull tight with glee,
These threads of our stories, unravelling free.

In the fabric of life, we stitch up our fate,
With goofball shenanigans that we celebrate.
A slip of a stitch, a yarn gone astray,
Yet each little trip leads us back to play.

With playful colors, we mark our delight,
In the quilt of our friendship, we shine, oh so bright.
Each patch a memory, sewn tight to the last,
In this tapestry woven, we hold the past.

So here's to the threads that bring us together,
In a world of nonsense, we'll always endeavor.
With silly tales woven, forever we'll stay,
In this crazy connection, we laugh all the way.

Charms of Memory

My wrist is home to tiny tales,
A spoon, a shoe, and even some snails.
Each charm jangles, sings a tune,
Did I wear this to lunch or the moon?

A cactus charm that pricks some pride,
Reminds me of the party outside.
A donut that's sweeter than any date,
Worn to a feast where I overate!

There's one that's shaped like a cat in a hat,
It's a story of meeting a very cool brat.
I wear my memories in jingles and gleams,
Who knew that wristwear could dance with dreams?

So if you see me sporting this art,
Know each little piece is a tickle to the heart.
With laughter and love, my wrist tells it true,
In charms and fun, I find pieces of you.

Intertwined Hearts

Two hearts twirl, then twist, then twine,
Like spaghetti getting lost in a line.
These trinkets shine, like secrets in night,
A pair gone waltzing, oh what a sight!

One's got a heart shaped like a bumblebee,
Buzzing with tales of you and me.
The other's a shoe, for dancing all night,
Worn out from stories of love and delight.

We laugh as they jingle, a happy parade,
Each jingle a laugh, each laugh, a cascade.
My wrist tells a story, wild and free,
A narrative woven just you and me.

The colors clash, like socks in a drawer,
But each little bling is worth so much more.
We're a funny love tale, let it unfurl,
In twinkling charms, we spin and we twirl!

Pieces of You and Me

A pizza charm that I can't resist,
Reminds me of nights that wrapped us in bliss.
A taco that wobbles, full of delight,
Each bite was a laugh 'til the morning light.

Here's a heart that sparkles, but not quite alive,
It giggles and dances, comes ready to thrive.
A tiny book charms my storytelling spree,
With tales of adventure, just you and me.

Do I have a charm that's a pair of old socks?
Oh yes, that's a memory, who cares if it blocks?
We danced in the rain, soaked down to our toes,
With laughter and love as the only prose.

So I gather those pieces, both silly and sweet,
Worn on my wrist, they dance with my beat.
In charming collection, my memories blend,
With the quirks of my life around every bend.

Circle of Secrets

In a circle of charms, secrets reside,
Like whispers in shadows, they giggle and hide.
A key to unlock all the quirks of our past,
Ready to burst forth, a fun-loving blast!

There's a fish charm that flops in despair,
Recalling the day that we lost our fair share.
A clock with no hands laughs time away,
Perfect for moments where we go astray.

A little balloon floats high in the sky,
Each laugh that we shared makes it soar up high.
A lightning bolt, for the zaps of surprise,
Each jolt brings a giggle, with wide-open eyes.

So wear it with joy, and never with fright,
This circle of secrets is pure delight.
For in charms we wear, we hold tight the jest,
In laughter we're bound, and here's to the best!

Winding Pathways of Passion

On this winding road we roam,
Laughing loud, we call it home.
With silly charms that jingle bright,
We dance together, pure delight.

In a market of tangled dreams,
I traded my snacks for wild schemes.
You wore my heart like a dainty crown,
While I tripped over shoelaces down.

Each twist and turn brings more surprise,
Like finding joy in a pair of ties.
Your giggles are the sweetest sound,
In this maze where fun is found.

We'll adorn our lives in carefree glee,
Like matching socks on a wild spree.
Together we'll dance, jump, and play,
In pathways of passions, come what may.

Emblazoned with Emotion

On sunny days, we paint the skies,
With colors only known to our eyes.
Crazy doodles on our hands,
We're the artists of our own lands.

Our laughter pops like bubble gum,
As we skip to the beat of a funky drum.
With makeshift crowns made of tinfoil,
We navigate through laughter's toil.

Each quirk and quibble, a treasure foretold,
With a pinch of humor, we're never too old.
Our chests adorned with stickers and flair,
We strut our stuff, without a care!

In our kingdom of silliness, we rule,
With quirky logic and plenty of drool.
Emblazoned with joy, we'll wear our charms,
Forever wrapped in each other's arms.

Tapestry of Together

We weave our lives with colorful yarn,
Stitching memories that make us laugh and bourn.
Each knot a giggle, each loop a cheer,
In this tapestry, you're my dear.

With threads of gold and shades of blue,
You sew the patches, I'll stitch for you.
Together we'll craft a masterpiece,
Creating joy that will never cease.

Your quirks add flair, like patches bright,
While I dance around in silly delight.
In our fabric of fun, we find our place,
Embroidered smiles on an endless face.

So here's to the weave of our design,
A playful bond that's simply divine.
With every twist, our joy will sing,
In this tapestry, love is the king.

Fragments of Forever

In a world of puzzles, we fit just right,
Two silly pieces of pure delight.
We chase the sun, our spirits bold,
Trading secrets, treasures untold.

With whispers shared and jokes so fine,
We craft a legacy, one that'll shine.
Each laugh a fragment, a tale to tell,
In this crazy journey where we excel.

Our memories sparkle, like stars at night,
Turning hiccups into pure delight.
We dance like no one is watching us roam,
In a shell of love, we've made our home.

So here's to the bits that tie us tight,
In fragments of forever, love takes flight.
Through every adventure, we'll gleefully go,
With a bond crafted in glitter and glow.

A Tapestry of Affection

We gather round, our links so bright,
With charms that jingle, what a sight!
Like silly ducks in a conga line,
Our goofy smiles, oh how they shine!

Each knot a joke, each twist a grin,
A playful dance, where we all win.
Our laughter echoes, a joyful tune,
Like silly cats under a full moon!

We giggle and tease, with love so true,
Tangled together, just me and you.
In this crazy weave, we find our cheer,
A colorful mess we hold so dear!

So let us twirl in this colorful thread,
With goofy antics, nothing to dread.
For every loop, a world we create,
In this tapestry, love's truly first rate!

Threads of Heartstrings

We stitched a bond, oh what a laugh,
Twirling yarn like a crazy giraffe!
With every tug, a silly shake,
We tie ourselves up for friendship's sake!

Each thread we pull, a story we share,
Like clowns on unicycles, flying through air.
Our smiles are bright, as we throw some shade,
In this tangled web, no plans need be made!

We craft our tales with a wink and a nudge,
While mismatched socks form our own grudge.
We laugh till we snort, no time for regret,
In this whimsical world, we've no need to fret!

So hop on this ride of thread and cheer,
With every twist, our friendship is clear.
In the circus of life, we wear our pride,
On this funny adventure, side by side!

Adorned in Affection

On this wrist, a jolly charm,
A rubber chicken—and oh, the farm!
With every jingle, a story unfolds,
Of dance parties where no one is old!

With googly eyes and a smile that winks,
We wear our quirks, and give crazy blinks.
Each piece we sport spins tales anew,
Of my pet goldfish who loves to chew!

Fashion choices that make us roar,
Like mismatched socks, we truly explore.
Adorned in laughter, we strut with pride,
In this playful outfit, there's nothing to hide!

So raise your glasses, let's toast to fun,
To wild adventures, and silly puns.
In this shimmery world where we spin and sway,
Our odd adornments brighten the day!

Chains of Togetherness

We're linked together like peas in a pod,
Chasing our tails, oh how we nod!
With chains of laughter, we wear our glee,
Like puppies dressed up for a grand spree!

Each link a chuckle, a joyful sound,
In this goofy train, love knows no bound.
With smiley faces and silly hats,
We dance in circles, like playful cats!

Through ups and downs, we hold on tight,
Rolling in laughter, our spirits in flight.
With every turn, we circle the sun,
In this chain of joy, we've already won!

So let's clasp our hands and dance about,
With chains of fun; let's shout and pout!
In this bond we share, there's nothing we lack,
Together forever, there's no turning back!

Bands of Belonging

On my wrist, a rainbow hue,
Sparkles bright, it's no big to-do.
Friends all laughing, what a sight,
This bling's got flair, it's pure delight.

Slap it on, and hear the cheer,
A bangle brigade, we commandeer.
With every shake, a jingle sings,
Who knew love came with so many rings?

Mismatched colors, what a mess,
But hey, it's stylish, I must confess.
Each charm tells tales, a silly song,
In this wacky world, we all belong.

So gather 'round, let's make a ruckus,
With wrist-bound dreams, we won't be what's rutless.
A goofy party, let's dance and sway,
With these silly bands, we'll laugh away!

Tokens of Tenderness

A piece of string, bright as a kite,
Made with love, it's quite the sight.
A twist, a turn, a giggle, a grin,
It's our little secret, let the games begin!

We trade our trinkets, with laughter we share,
Dancing through life without a care.
My heart's on my sleeve, yours on my wrist,
With these funny gifts, it'll be hard to miss.

Did you see that one? It jingles loud!
A token of tenderness, we make ourselves proud.
We prance and parade, with flair and fun,
Together forever, we're never outdone.

So, let's stack them high, till they start to wobble,
With each little token, we'll burst into gobble.
A funny little ritual, we'll never outgrow,
In this silly love game, we steal the show!

Adornment of Affection

On my wrist, a tiny zoo,
Sparkly critters, they wave to you.
A lion roars, a monkey swings,
Look at my charms, oh what fun bling!

Each piece a laugh, each giggle a cheer,
With these adornments, there's nothing to fear.
From hearts to stars, they jive and dance,
Who knew trinkets could lead to romance?

Let's barter bracelets, trade with a wink,
For every swap, we rethink our link.
A silly conflict? Just laugh it away,
With each adornment, come join the fray!

So, wear your joy like a badge of pride,
With our playful bling, we'll take it in stride.
In this whimsical world, we humorously sway,
With our adornments of affection, we'll brighten the day!

Unbreakable Bonds

Wrist to wrist, we build our crew,
With strings of laughter, nothing feels blue.
A clasp of chaos, a twist of fate,
In our unbreakable bonds, we celebrate!

These wobbly charms make quite the noise,
Together we shine, oh what joys!
Fuzzy feelings, silly dreams,
Our love's a cartoon, bursting at the seams!

With tangled threads, and colors galore,
We're weaving memories, always wanting more.
Come join the fun, let's frolic and play,
With our unbreakable bonds, we'll never sway!

So rally your friends, let's make a row,
In this joyful dance, we steal the show.
With every jingle, we laugh and respond,
In this cherished circle, we're forever bond!

Love's Unseen Patterns

In a drawer full of odds and ends,
There lies a treasure that never bends.
A twisted piece of gummy rope,
It holds together, our wildest hope.

We laugh at the charms that never fit,
And wonder, will this ever quit?
The shapes and colors dance in glee,
A puzzle missing half its spree.

From macaroni to paper clips,
Each trinket tells of playful trips.
Worn on weekends, a fashion crime,
But what's a little glue at this time?

So here's to ties that make us smile,
Crafted with love, with a silly style.
Who needs shiny gems from afar?
When our hearts sparkle like a candy jar.

Ties of Time

We've got some string from '98,
Tangled memories, isn't that great?
A knotted mess of moments past,
Yet somehow these bonds hold fast.

The fashion police may want to call,
But love's not about a glittery thrall.
With shoelaces and more, we're bound,
In this crazy world, we dance around.

A friendship band, a lanyard too,
It's all a part of me and you.
Wrapped 'round our wrists, like silly jokes,
Creating joy in the hearts of folks.

So let's tie knots that even unravel,
And wear them proudly through this travel.
For every twist and every turn,
Love's intricate dance is what we yearn.

Strands of Affection

With yarn so bright, I weave and spin,
A masterpiece that's sure to win.
An ugly sweater might come to play,
But love's true colors never sway.

Little beads that don't quite match,
Yet somehow they form the perfect patch.
A wobbly heart that looks askew,
Just like my feelings for you, it's true!

In every loop, there's laughter laced,
As we wear our heart, a masked-faced.
Fuzzy tales on wrists we share,
Like stories told without a care.

So let's embrace this woven art,
Crafted with the goofiest heart.
For in these strands, our love will shine,
A tapestry of silly, so divine.

Crafts of the Heart

With glue sticks and glitter all around,
We create wonders without a sound.
A paper heart, a gemless ring,
Silly gifts, the joy they bring!

The craft fair called, 'We won't be missed',
With macaroni, we craft our tryst.
Friends and lovers all in a row,
Stick it together, let the laughter flow.

Tiny hands make giant dreams,
Pulling threads of friendship beams.
With each crafted piece, our hearts unfold,
More precious than diamonds, if truth be told.

So gather your scraps, let's make it fun,
In this crafter's paradise, we have won.
For in every mess, a love appears,
Crafted with joy, surpassing all fears.

Tinsel of Togetherness

When we laugh, the world spins fast,
Like tangled yarn, our worries passed.
Your quirks shine bright, a giddy sight,
My heart's a dance; oh, what a night!

A bangle's jingle, a playful tease,
We twirl like leaves in the summer breeze.
With every twist, our stories bloom,
In this wild circus, we clear the gloom.

We trade our secrets, and silly vows,
Like mismatched socks and crazy cows.
With each odd charm, our tale expands,
Life's just more fun when chaos lands!

Together we hover with mischief rampant,
Counting the rings from our sweet enchantment.
In this jesting world, we craft our way,
Creating laughter, come what may!

Caressed by Color

In shades of blue and bright cerulean,
We paint our lives, like a fine chameleon.
Your love's a splash, a vibrant spree,
Like confetti tossed, wild and free!

A rainbow twist to our daily grind,
With every hue, a new joy we find.
Polka dots dance on my favorite dress,
In this colorful chaos, we're truly blessed.

With silly hats and mismatched shoes,
Life's a canvas, no way to lose!
Each joke a brushstroke, a laugh a spark,
Lighting our path in the wild, dark park.

Drenched in laughter and draped in cheer,
Creating memories, one silly tear.
In this kaleidoscope, let us remain,
For every color sings love's refrain!

Love's Woven Tapestry

In threads of gold and layers of glee,
Our mishaps weave into great history.
Your laughter loops in every design,
With a stitch of charm, our lives align.

Bit by bit, we gather the bits,
From goofy pranks to our funny fits.
Each fiber tells a tale so bright,
In this wacky quilt, everything's right.

We tug at seams, a comical fight,
You pull my leg; I pull your light.
Through tangled yarns and knots so tight,
Together we soar, what a delight!

Each patch a moment in wild embrace,
In this quirky art, we find our place.
With every twist and each playful spin,
Our tapestry glows, we yarn with a grin!

Elegance Enshrined

In posh ball gowns and fancy shoes,
We dance like we've got nothing to lose.
Your clumsy twirls, my dashing glide,
A royal affair on this silly ride.

With feather boas and sparkling bling,
Who knew elegance could make us swing?
You told a joke, I nearly fell,
In this grand ball, we weave our spell.

Amidst the laughter, a dash of flair,
We toast with cookies; oh, what a pair!
With every step, our hearts align,
In this riotous waltz, love's clearly fine.

Dressed to the nines, yet oh, so fun,
We shine like stars when the day is done.
With elegance wrapped in a happy swirl,
Here's to the joy in this crazy whirl!

Ties That Bind

In a drawer they clatter and jingle,
Like loyal friends sighing to mingle.
A twist here, a snap there, oh what a sight,
They dance on our wrists, bringing sheer delight.

They stretch and they pull, a comic ballet,
Promising style on a budget today.
With colors that pop, each one a surprise,
Who knew arm candy could reach such highs?

They snag on the door, then tangle with hair,
A game of tug-of-war, do we really care?
Each clasp a reminder of laughter we share,
Even when we look silly, we wear them with flair.

So here's to the chaos and glitter they bring,
Each twist and each turn, it makes our hearts sing.
Though quirky and wild, our love stays entwined,
With every mishap, our fate's well aligned.

Echoes of Embrace

With jingles and jangles, they sing on our arms,
A playful parade of decorative charms.
In coffee shops buzzing, they clink with a cheer,
A symphony of love that tickles the ear.

Each missing link tells of stories gone wild,
Like that time at the fair when the ferris wheel smiled.
They spark laughter loud, as we dance without care,
Bracelets of mischief, floating in air.

Adorned with odd bling, they shine just the same,
As we giggle and guffaw, no need to feel shame.
They twist and they tangle, a comical mess,
Each knot a confession, we love to impress.

With each little snap, hear the punchlines arise,
In this circus of life, they're the ultimate prize.
So grab all your friends, let's wind up the fun,
Together we shine, like the moon and the sun.

Enchanted Adornments

Oh what a spectacle these trinkets inspire,
With beads and bright colors, their glow never tires.
Adventures await on our wrists they create,
Clinking in rhythm, our love's some great fate.

A clasp on my sweater, oh what a surprise,
I trip on these treasures, how they tease my eyes.
Each bling tells a tale, a reminder so sweet,
That every misstep is a dance on repeat.

They fly like confetti with each little sway,
Creating a ruckus, come join in the play!
When we wear our stories, the laughter ignites,
What fun it can be under starry, bright nights.

So hold on to this chaos, let's twist and let spin,
Each mishap a memory where love can begin.
With giggles and grins, this charm won't evade,
In this whimsical world, our hearts are not weighed.

Love's Layered Craft

In piles on the dresser, a colorful mound,
Like misfit toys waiting to be found.
Each piece holds a secret, a wink and a grin,
The laughter, the moments, they wear from within.

It jingles and jangles through life's crazy ride,
Where some parts may fade but the laughter won't hide.
With a twist and a knot, how they sparkle and shine,
These bits of enchantment, always divine.

A slip on the wrist, then a tumble or fall,
A giggle escapes at our clumsy recall.
With each sparkly glance, there's a story to sow,
Through every mischief, our love's sure to grow.

So wear them with pride, let each moment unfold,
With laughter as gold, and treasures untold.
In this vibrant parade, let's uplift and embrace,
As we wrap up our love in this whimsical space.

Links of Longing

Across the wrist I see a spark,
A pastry chef with flour and lark.
She tied a knot, a colorful twist,
Said, 'Join my dance, you can't resist!'

A cow in boots jumped high and wide,
With candy arms, she did abide.
These silly links, they cheer me so,
In every hue, they steal the show!

The postman grinned, oh what a sight,
Delivering dreams in colors bright.
He tossed them high with a funny flair,
Said, 'Catch these giggles if you dare!'

So here we twirl with jingling sound,
The comedy of love we've found.
In every clasp, a story flows,
A tune of laughter, as it glows!

Emotions Etched in Time

A timepiece tangled on my wrist,
Tick-tock giggles that can't be missed.
With every tick, a wink so sly,
Time plays tricks, and I won't lie!

Enchanted charms with faces bright,
A tiny chef sways left and right.
Heart-shaped pasta, I caught a glance,
Jumping joyfully in a dance!

Each bead a tale of ups and downs,
Like silly clowns in vibrant gowns.
They poke and prod, at every turn,
In this wild ride, I gladly learn!

So let's embrace this funny spree,
With whimsy, laughter, wild and free.
Etched in time, with every laugh,
A joyful heart is the best craft!

Ties of Trust

With ribbons bright there hangs a tale,
Of goats in socks set to unveil.
Each twist and turn, a joke to share,
Trusting friends, we laugh without care.

Their silly faces perched in pairs,
Like oopsie daisies caught unawares.
We tie our tales in knots so tight,
A tapestry of joyful delight!

In every clasp, a wink or frown,
Under green skies and fluffy brown.
With every chuckle, we craft our fate,
These bonds of friendship, oh how great!

So here's to ties that never fray,
In this charming, funny ballet.
Each giggle shared, a new thread spun,
Life's merry dance has just begun!

Charm of the Heart

A tiny charm, it jiggles bright,
Winks from the wrist, what a sight!
With every jingle, joy takes flight,
A whimsical dance in the moonlight.

The jester's cap tips off with glee,
Spins a yarn, just wait and see.
A donut hops on a midnight train,
Bringing with it the joys and plain!

In silly shapes, my treasures gleam,
Like shrimp in hats, they make me beam.
With every laugh, a bond is born,
As day breaks in, the world adorned.

So here's to charms and laughter grand,
Hand in hand, we take a stand.
For life's a joke, a playful art,
In every smile, the charm of heart!

www.ingramcontent.com/pod-product-compliance
Lightning Source LLC
Chambersburg PA
CBHW070006300426
43661CB00141B/263